THE ARENA OF TIGLATH-PILESER III'S CAMPAIGN AGAINST SARDURI II (743 B.C.)

Michael C. Astour
Southern Illinois University at Edwardsville

In 743 B.C., Tiglath-pileser III led a victorious march against Sarduri II of Urarṭu and his vassals. A comparison of the four extant Assyrian relations of that campaign yields a clear picture of its geographical arena. Unfortunately, Waldemar Belck, in 1904, utterly confused this picture by his identifications of two battlegrounds, Kištam and Ḫalpi, with modern Küştam and Halfeti. These were uncritically followed by generations of scholars, and can still be found in serious publications. This paper, based on Assyrian and Urarṭian records, as well as on the study of the natural relief and road connections of the region in question, proposes a different reconstruction of Tiglath-pileser III's line of advance and of the battlegrounds along it.

Table of Contents

> Military plans are influenced by various factors, economic, political or tactical in character. Even so, the determining considerations have their ultimate basis in the physical features of the areas; troop movements are largely regulated by topography, even as the growth of civilization and the pattern of population distribution conform to the direction in which rivers flow and the way in which goods are transported to markets at the least cost.
>
> S.L.A. Marshall, *The American Heritage History of World War I* (1966 ed.), 64.

1. Urarṭian Expansion under Menua and Argišti

When Tiglath-pileser III seized the throne in 745, Assyria had been steadily losing ground to the vigorously expanding Kingdom of Urarṭu. Beginning with Menua (ca. 805-788), the kings of Urarṭu succeeded in pushing back the northern boundary of the Assyrian Empire and in virtually encircling it on its eastern and western flanks.[1] In the west, Assyria claimed overlordship over Northern Syria and Melitene (kingdom of Melid) in Anatolia since Ashurnasirpal II and Shalmaneser III. But Menua, the contemporary of Adad-nirari III, conquered Alzi on the upper Tigris (which was still part of an Assyrian province in 799),[2] Ḫulmeri/Qulmeri (Assyrian Kullimeri, Byzantine Chlomarôn), Šebeteria (now Palu), Ḫuzana (Byzantine Chozana, now Hozat), Ṣupā (Hittite and Assyrian Ṣuppa, classical Sophene), and reached the border of the "Hittite Land" (^{KUR}*Ḫa-ti-na*, ^{KUR}*Ḫa-a-ti-i-na-a*),[3] as the Urarṭians called Anatolia west of the Euphrates. He did not have to cross the river in order to receive tribute from the "Meliṭeian king" (MAN ^{URU}*Me-li-ṭè-i-a-al-ḫé*).[4] Menua's successor, Argišti I (787-766), probably in his fourth regnal year, undertook a short victorious campaign against Ḫilaruada, king of Melid, in which thousands of inhabitants were carried off and resettled near the northeastern border of Urarṭu.[5] The next king, Sarduri II (765-733),[6]

[1] The chronology of the kings of Urarṭu is approximate, but the margin of variance between different scholars is not wide. The dates given here are those used by Garelli and Nikiprowetzky (1974), 101-102, 105. Urarṭian royal inscriptions are cited according to their numeration in both Melikišvili (1960) (siglum: UKN) and König (1955) (siglum: HCI).

[2] Stele No. 39 of Marduk-ḪAL-ani, eponym of 799; cf. Ungnad *RLA* II, 439; Forrer (1920), 29; Diakonoff (1968), 156 n. 209. Menua's conquest of ^{KUR}*Al-z*[*i*]*-i-ni-ni*: UKN 28, obv. 8 (HCI 16,IX, 8). Alzi is the classical Arzanene.

[3] The former spelling occurs in UKN 28, obv. 7 (HCI 16,IX,7), the latter in UKN 39, 11 (HCI, IV, 11). *-na* is an omissible plural suffix (Salvini [1972], 102); in several other Urarṭian inscriptions the name is written without it. The occurrence of the suffixed form caused the erroneous identification of Menua's Ḫatina with the state of Ḫattina in the Plain of Antioch, as in Burney and Lang (1972), 136. Menua never penetrated into Syria; besides, the alleged *Ḫattina* was actually read *Pat(t)inu* (Hawkins [1974], 81 and n. 99).

[4] UKN 39, 16 (HCI 25, IV, 16). The Urarṭian suffix *-alḫi/ḫali* served to create ethnic adjectives (Melikišvili [1960], 52). In the preceding line, [?]*-su-li-e-ḫa-ú-a-li* is taken as the personal name of the king of Meliṭea by König (1955), 64 n. 7; Laroche (1966), 164 No. 1167; Garelli and Nikiprowetzky (1974), 101 (misprinted *Suliehanali*). This is denied by Melikišvili (1960), 162; cf. also Hawkins (1974), 76.

[5] UKN 127, II, 5-24 (HCI 80, §. 3).

[6] This monarch is designated as Sarduri II in Soviet works on Urarṭu, as well as by S.Smith (1925), 31;

early in his reign, launched a new attack against this same Ḫilaruada, or perhaps his homonymous grandson.[7] This campaign is described, besides a damaged passage of Sarduri II's annals,[8] in the westernmost of all extant Urarṭian inscriptions, carved on a cliff over the left bank of the Euphrates and referred to as either the Kömürhan or the Izolu inscription (from the names of the towns at the nearby Euphrates crossings), but actually located near the village of Hatipuşaği, 3 km. upstream from the modern bridge at Kömürhan.[9]

The launching point of the expedition was the town Ṭumeški[10] (^{URU}*Ṭu-me-iš-ki*). It is also mentioned in the same inscription as one of the nine fortresses annexed to Urarṭu by Sarduri II.[11] Since all of them seem to have been located on the left bank of the Euphrates,[12] and since the Hatipuşaği inscription stands in the middle of a ruined Urarṭian stronghold,[13] M. Salvini is certainly right in reviving and substantiating the old idea[14] that the name *Ṭumeški* survived in the first century B.C. as *Tomisa*, a fortress in Sophene, across the river from the kingdom of Cappadocia (which at that time included Melitene) and on the highway from Mazaca (Kayseri) to the regions east of the Euphrates,[15] and that Ṭumeški-Tomisa corresponds to the ruined castle near Hatipuşagi which dominates the old road from Malatya to Elâziğ.[16] As for the military operations against Ḫilaruada, they certainly took place west of the Euphrates.[17] Sarduri speaks about the investment and surrender of the city itself of Meliṭea,[18] and out of the five

Sayce (1925), 176; Gurney (1954), 45; Schmökel (1957), 259; Burney and Lang (1972), 147-50; Salvini (1972), 102; van Loon (1974), 187 n. 2; but as Sarduri III by Belck (1904), 182-3; Forrer (1920), 31, 56; Bossert (1951), 63; König (1955), 1, 19; Goetze (1957), 192; Roux (1966), 275, 279; Garelli and Nikiprowetzky (1974), 105-6. There is no proof that Sarduri, son of Argišti, was preceded on the throne by more than one namesake.

7 The king of Meliṭea is called Ḫilaruada, son of Šaḫu, by Sarduri II, UKN 158, 2 (HCI 104, I, 2); no patronymic is given by Argišti. It is not impossible that Argišti's adversary was still alive some 25 years later (Melikišvili [1960], 429); but Salvini (1972), 102 considers it unlikely.

8 UKN 156, B, I (HCI 102, rev. VI).

9 UKN 158 (HCI 104); also published by Beran (1957) and van Loon (1974), who calls the village by its alternate name Habibuşagi. On its exact location see Salvini (1972) 107.

10 Line 11. Van Loon (1974) recognized a mention of the Euphrates (^{ID}*Pu-ra-na-di*) in a difficult passage, line 6. According to this interpretation, Sarduri claimed to have been the first king to cross it; but what about Argišti I?

11 Lines 24-31. We must abstain from discussing the names and possible locations of eight out of these nine fortresses as being only of marginal importance to our topic.

12 Diakonoff (1968), 161 and n. 228; Salvini (1972) 107-08.

13 Cf. Burney and Lang (1972), 135; "At Komurhan stands the westernmost Urartian fortress, with a rock inscription of Sarduri II. This was a frontier post, little now remains of the walls; significantly the pottery there . . . is of Urartian type."

14 For which he credits (p. 109 and nn. 23 and 24) W. Tomaschek *ap. H. Kiepert Festschrift* (Berlin 1898), 137.

15 Strabo XII, 2, 1; XIV, 2, 29; also mentioned by Stephanus Byzantius *s.v.* as a "border-town of Cappadocia near the Taurus."

16 Salvini (1972), 107-10, with ample references to pertaining literature.

17 Diakonoff (1968), 161 n. 228 asserts that "the text does not indicate that Sardur II crossed the Euphrates," which contradicts the plain meaning of the text even without van Loon's finding there of the very name of the Euphrates (n. 10 above).

18 Now the mound of Arslantepe 7 km. (by road) from modern Malatya.

other localities of Ḫilaruada's domain mentioned in the Hatipuşaği inscription, three can be identified with places in or near Melitene.[19] Thus Melitene was forced into the zone of Urarṭian domination, and for fifty years Assyria did nothing to recover this remote dependency.[20]

2. Sarduri II's Expeditions to Niḫiria and Kummuḫ

But Adad-nirari III and his successors did not relinquish their claims to Northern Syria, which included the states of Kummuḫ, Gurgum, Sam'al, Carchemish, Arpad, Patinu (Unqi), and the dual kingdom of Hamath and Hadrach (Ḫatarikka). In several campaigns, Adad-nirari III was able to re-establish the Assyrian sovereignty over the Syrian states which had been lost under his father Šamši-Adad V.[21] Adad-nirari III's weak successors still conducted expeditions to Syria: Shalmaneser IV went to the Cedar Mountain (Amanus) in 775,[22] and against Damascus in 773, though five of his regnal years (781, 780, 779, 778, and 776) are marked "against Urarṭu" in the Eponym Canon;[23] Aššur-dân III, in a time of turmoil and plague in Assyria, launched three attacks on the break-away Ḫatarikka (in 772, 765, and 755); and Aššur-nirari V, in his first year of reign (754), marched on Arpad and re-imposed a treaty of vassalage on its king Mati'-ilu.[24] But this was all the weakened Assyria could undertake at that juncture. Soon afterward, in 753 or 752,[25] Sarduri II made a daring move on the central Assyrian

19 The mountain land of Karniše corresponds to the mountain (land) of Karna, KBo I 1 obv. I 12, 21 (cf. Garstang and Gurney [1959], 40-1), and to Kornê (Corne) of Roman times, 8 Roman miles (12 km.) from the city of Melitene towards the Euphrates. The "royal city" (district capital) of Sasi may correspond to Zaz(z)iša, KBo I 1 obv. I, 11, 20, KBo III 4 rev. III 69, and elsewhere in the Boğazköy texts (cf. Garstang and Gurney [1959], 32). The land of Mušanie reminds one of Miasena or Mesena, 12 Roman miles (18 km.) from Melitene on the road to Samosata, located by Honigmann (1954), 37 and Map II, at or near Kuyulu.

20 Melid is not mentioned in the extant records of Adad-nirari III and his successors. It participated in the Syro-Anatolian coalition against the pro-Assyrian Zakur of Hamath according to the latter's Aramaic inscription, and must have been one of the rebel states of the Ḫatti land defeated by Adad-nirari III early in his reign (cf. the fragmentary inscription published by Millard and Tadmor [1973], 58). Melidians ([KUR]*Me-li-d*[*a*]*-a-a*) appear in lists of wine allocations to members of the Assyrian royal court at Kalaḫ and to foreigners (Kinnier Wilson [1972], text 6:52); the latter, as seen by Tadmor (1975), 42 were not captives but visiting merchants or ambassadors. These lists date from the first quarter of the eighth century.

21 On Adad-nirari III's Syrian campaigns cf.: Page (1968); Donner (1970); Oded (1972); Millard and Tadmor (1973); Tadmor (1973). A stele of Adad-nirari III, with an added inscription of Shalmaneser IV, was recently found at Pazarcik (near Maraş). Pending its publication, one learns from Hawkins (1973), 309, 311, (1974), 74-5, 80, and his article in *RLA* IV (1973), 157, that it tells of Adad-nirari's help to Kummuḫ against Gurgum and his fixation of the boundary between them. Another inscription, discovered near Antakya, as I was kindly told by J. D. Hawkins, tells of another border arbitration by Adad-nirari III, this time between Arpad and Hamath.

22 One would think that it was at that opportunity that he added his own inscription to that of his father at Pazarcik, but it also speaks of the turtan Šamši-ilu's expedition against Damascus, probably the one mentioned in the Eponym Canon under 773.

23 The last of these years is annotated "against Urarṭu (and) Namri" (in the Zagros).

24 Text, German translation, and commentary: Weidner (1933). English translations: *ARAB* I,§ . 749-60; E. Reiner *ap. ANET*[3], 532-3.

front. After defeating two kings on the northeastern frontier of Urarṭu, Sarduri (or, in his phraseology, the god Ḫaldi) "vanquished Aššur-nirari, son of Adad-nirari, king of Assyria, vanquished the land of Arme, vanquished the city of Niḫiria, its royal city, threw them down before Sarduri, son of Argišti."[26] The wording of this passage shows that the land of Arme and its "royal city" (district capital) Niḫiria were part of Assyrian territory. Niḫiria, or Niḫria, is amply attested in geographical contexts in Old Assyrian, Mariote, Middle Assyrian, and Hittite texts, which indicate that it was identical with Amida/Diyarbakır on the Tigris. It was renamed *Amedi* by the Arameans who established there a state in the tenth century (hence *Arme*), but the Urarṭians continued to call it by its traditional name.[27] It was an Assyrian province since Shalmaneser III. Sarduri's annals do not indicate that he tried to hold the city for good, but the very fact that Aššur-nirari did not react to the raid[28] was symptomatic. Emboldened by Assyria's passivity, Sarduri expanded his kingdom to the north and east, and around 746 or 745 turned westward and invaded Northern Syria.

His target was the kingdom which he called *Qumaḫa*[29] and the Assyrians *Kum(m)uḫu*, the Greco-Roman Commagene, south of the Taurus from the previously subdued Melitene. It was ruled at that time by Kuštašpili (Kuštašpi of Tiglath-pileser III's annals) who had never recognized the overlordship of Urarṭu. "The gods opened me the road," says Sarduri: "Hastily? I marched against the land of Qumaḫa. Uita (^{URU}*Ú-i-ta-ni*), a royal city, a fortified one, I conquered in battle. Ḫalpa (^{URU}*Ḫa-al-pa-ni*), a royal city, located on a lake (*ṣu-i-ni-i-ši-ni*), I conquered. Parala (^{URU}*Pa-ra-la-ni*), a royal city, I captured?. He[30] came before me, prostrated himself, I lifted him up, he gave me tribute: 40 minas of pure? gold, 800 minas of silver, 3000 garments, 2000 copper shields, 1535 copper bowls . . ." As recognized by Melikišvili,[31] the first of the captured cities, Uita, is identical with ^{URU}*Ú-e-ta-áš*, a "royal city" of Lalla, king of Melid, which Shalmaneser III took in 836.[32] The city was thus located on the border between Melid and Kummuḫ, on the plateau of the Taurus traversed by the only road linking the two regions which is fit for wheel traffic, and where there are several ruined as well as inhabited sites.[33] Border shifts between neighboring states were quite common in

25 Thus approximately dated by Melikišvili (1960), 300, on the ground of the relative position of the passage in Sarduri II's annals.

26 UKN 156, D, I (HCI 102, right side, I).

27 The framework of this article does not allow us to adduce and interpret the inscriptional evidence on Niḫiria/Niḫria.

28 The years 753-750 are marked "in the land" in the Eponym Canon.

29 It appears in his annals (UKN 155, E, 35, 41, 48 = HCI 103, 9, 43, 47, 54) with the ethnic adjectival suffix -*ḫali*/-*alḫi*, as, respectively, ^{KUR}*Qu-ma-ḫa-li-i*, ^{KUR}*Qu-ma-ḫa-al-ḫi-*[*e*], and ^{KUR}*Qu-ma-ḫa-ḫa-li-ni-*⌜*e*⌝.

30 The pronoun refers to Kuštašpili, king of Kumaḫa, mentioned previously, line 41 (HCI: 47).

31 Melikišvili (1960), 445; accepted by Diakonoff (1968), 161 and n. 230.

32 *ARAB* I 580. In the inscription on a statue of Shalmaneser III from Nimrud, fragment F (Laessøe [1959], 155), ^{URU}*Ú-e-*[*ta-áš*] is called "a fortress of Lalla the Melidian," whence Shalmaneser III proceeded to ^{URU}*Ta-ga-ri-*[..]. We restore the last sign as [*ma*]; *Tagarima* (thus to be read also in RS 16,114, rev. 3, instead of Nougayrol's *Ta-ga-ri-la*?) is identical with Hittite *Tegarama*, biblical *Togarmah*, and later Assyrian (Sargonid) *Til-Garimmu*, a major city of the kingdom of Melid-Kammanu, usually identified with Gürün, but more probably located closer to the city of Melid, perhaps at Akçadağ (formerly Arga, classical Arca).

33 Sürgü, Alni Harab, Doğanşehir, Harabşehir, Muhacirler, Çiklik (with a mound).

Northern Syria before its absorption into the Assyrian Empire. We shall deal further on with the location of the second city, Ḫalpa, and we limit ourselves at this stage to stating the obvious fact that since it belonged to the kingdom of Kummuḫ, it had nothing in common with its more famous namesake, Ḫalpa/Ḫalab (Aleppo).[34] The third city, Parala, is otherwise unknown, but it could not have been situated very far from the Taurus, because Sarduri stopped his advance before reaching the capital of Kummuḫ, which bore the same name as the kingdom and occupied the site of the later Samosata (now Samsat).[35]

The sequence of Sarduri II's annals says nothing of his further activities in Northern Syria. But the annals and other records of Tiglath-pileser III inform us that in 743 Sarduri was the overlord not only of Sulumal of Melid and of Kuštašpi of Kummuḫ, but also of two other kings, Tarḫulara of Gurgum and Matiʿ-ilu of Arpad (the same on whom Aššur-nirari V had imposed a vassal treaty eleven years earlier).[36] It does not seem that any other states of Syria became Urarṭian vassals. Bossert's attempt to identify a certain Sasturas (*Sa-sa-tu*$_4$*-ra-ś*), who is mentioned in two hieroglyphic Hittite inscriptions,[37] with Sarduri II, and to interpret the relevant passages as testifying to that king's sovereignty over Carchemish, is unfounded.[38] Nor is there any justification for Gurney's adding of Sam'al, Unqi, and Que (Eastern Cilicia) to the "adherents" of Urarṭu.[39] But even so, Sarduri's intrusion into Syria was an intolerable challenge to the

34 This remark may seem unnecessary, but the mistake is found with such scholars as Bittel (1950), 78: "Urartu extended . . . up to Halpa (Aleppo)," Bossert (1951), 63: "Sarduris III . . . turned against Aleppo," and Goetze (1957), 192: "Sardur III . . . conquered . . . Kumaḫa (Commagene) and Ḫalpa (Aleppo)."

35 The Assyrians referred to Kummuḫ as both a country and a city. An obvious location for the capital city is the very large mound at Samsat, one of the most impressive in all of Anatolia and Northern Syria, on which a hieroglyphic Hittite stele was found. Its identification with the city of Kummuḫ was accepted by Forrer (1920), 78-9; Ed. Meyer (1931), 370; Naster (1938), map; Hawkins (1970), 69. The Chaldean Chronicle (BM 22047, 13 = Wiseman [1956], 21 puts [URU]*Ki-mu-ḫu* on the west bank of the Euphrates; its identity with *Kum(m)uḫu* of the Assyrian texts was recognized by Albright (1956), 29.

36 The idea of Dupont-Sommer (1956), 39-41, that the mysterious *Br-G'yh*, king of *Ktk*, who appears in the Aramaic treaty from Sfireh as the suzerain of Matiʿ-ilu (*Mtʿʾl*) of Arpad, is none other than Sarduri II of Urarṭu, must be rejected on internal grounds. The treaty states that *Br-G'yh*'s domain abutted on the territory of Arpad since the days of his fathers. This is not true for Urarṭu. If *Br-G'yh* and *Ktk* are pseudonyms, then the simplest thing is to assume that they stand for Aššur-nirari and Assyria, as seen by Cantineau (1931). [The Editorial Board of *Assur* asked me to express my opinion of the recent proposal by A. Malamat (1976) to equate *Ktk* with URU*Ki*-x-[x]-*qa*, which appears once in Shalmaneser III's annals as a district town in the Mesopotamian part of Bīt-Adini. Even if the damaged sign(s) could be presumed to read *it*, and the use of *q* instead of *k* at the end of the name could be explained away, it would still be impossible for a provincial town east of the Euphrates, which at the time of the Sfireh treaty has for over a hundred years belonged to Assyria, to impose a vassal treaty upon the kingdom of Arpad.]

37 Meriggi (1967) No. 28 (inscr. from Čekkeh): (1975) No. 217 (inscr. A 20b-22 from Carchemish).

38 Bossert (1951), 63; also Houwink ten Cate (1967), 126. But the text of the Čekkeh stele contradicts this hypothesis, cf. Meriggi (1953), 34 n. 2, and Hawkins (1972), 104-05. J. D. Hawkins, in a section of his article "Some Historical Problems in the Hieroglyphic Luwian Inscriptions" (soon to appear in *AnSt*), offers a new interpretation of the Čekkeh stele, according to which Sasturas was "the first servant" (prime minister) of Kamanas, king of Carchemish.

39 Gurney (1954), 45. Cf. Lloyd (1956), 184 who speaks of "an Urartian prince who fought side by side with the Karatepe king [Awarikus/Urik of Que] against the Assyrians." There is no indication whatever that Urik resisted Tiglath-pileser III before paying him tribute in 738.

His first two regnal years[40] were devoted to expeditions into southern Mesopotamia (*birit nāri)* and against Namri, but in 743 he moved westward and put an end to the overlordship of Urarṭu not only in Northern Syria (where it did not exceed two or three years) but also in Melitene (where it began much earlier).

3. Tiglathileser III's Records on the Campaign of 743

Our knowledge of that campaign derives from the annotation for 743 in the Eponym Canon and from four separate relations in various records of Tiglath-pileser III which complement each other:

> 1. The Eponym Canon:[41] Tiglath-pileser, king of Assyria. In Arpad. A defeat on Urarṭu was inflicted.
>
> 2. Annals:[42] [In my third] year of reign, [Sardurri of Urarṭu revolted against me, . . . with] Mati'-ilu . . . [Sulumal of Melid], Tarḫulara of [Gurgum], [Kuštašpi of Kummuḫ], [trusted] in each others might. . . . (Trusting) in the might and power of Assur, my lord, I fought with them, . . . large numbers of them I slew. The gorges and precipices of mountains I filled with [their bodies]. Their chariots . . . their . . . without number, I carried away from that slaughter and of Sardurri . . . I seized with my own hands. 72,950 people, together with their possessions, from . . . [Sardurri], to save his life, escaped at night and was seen no more . . . up to the bridge across the Euphrates, the boundary of his land, I pursued him. (Here follows a description of the booty).
>
> 3. *Nimrud slab inscription*:[43] Sardaurri of Urarṭu revolted against me and made common cause with Mati'-ilu. In Kištan and Ḫalpi, districts of Kummuḫ (*i-na* ^{KUR}*Kiš-ta-*[*an ù*] ^{KUR}*Ḫal-pi na-gi-i ša* ^{URU}*Ku-mu-ḫi)* I defeated him and took from him the whole of his camp. He became

[40] Tiglath-pileser III's reckoning of his regnal years (*palû*) differed from the standard Assyrian postdating system. Normally, the year of his accession, 745, should have been referred to as "the beginning of the reign" rather than the first regnal year. He originally adhered to this tradition and took the eponymate in 743, his second full year of reign, as it was customary for Assyrian kings. But later on he counted his accession year as his first *palû*, and this numeration was followed in his annals.

[41] Ungnad in *RLA* II, 430.

[42] Rost (1892), pl. XIV. It is well known that the annals of Tiglath-pileser III survived in a very damaged state and that their publication by Rost is far from satisfactory, not the least because of the uncertain order of the component slabs. However, since the new critical edition of the annals by H. Tadmor, the principles of which he has expounded in (1967), has not appeared as of this writing, we must quote the relevant passage as it is translated in *ARAB* I, § 769, from Rost's edition.

[43] Rost (1892), pl. XXXIII; *ARAB* I, § 785; written in 734, or soon after.

> frightened at the fury of my arms and ran away, alone, to save his life.[44]
>
> 4. *Nimrud tablet:*[45] [Sarduri]⌜of Urarṭu⌝, Sulumal of Melid, Tarḫulara [of Gurgum]. . . Kuštašpi of Kummuḫ, to capture and plunder . . .between Kištan and Ḫalpi, districts of [Kummuḫ] ([*bi*]-*rit* ^KUR^*Kiš-ta-an ù* ^KUR^*Ḫal-pi na-gi-i ša* ^KUR^[*Ku-mu-ḫi*]), . . . them. The river Sinzi (^ÍD^*Si-in-zi*) I dyed red like wool . . . their . . . I took away from them. In the midst . . . his royal bed . . .
>
> 5. *Second Nimrud slab:*[46] Sarduri of Urarṭu revolted against me and made common cause with Mati'-ilu of Bīt-Agusi (DUMU ^m^*A-gu-us-si*). Between Kištan and Ḫalpi, districts of Kummuḫ, I defeated them. The whole of his camp I took from him. He became frightened at the awful brilliance of my arms and to save his life mounted a mare and escaped to Mount Sibag (^KUR^*Si-bag*), a steep mountain, at night, and ascended it.

The following preliminary conclusions can be drawn, on internal grounds, from the quoted documents: 1. The original goal of the expedition was Arpad, and the main culprit among Sarduri's allies was its king Matiʿ-ilu. In shorter versions, only he is mentioned by name. This agrees with the subsequent annotations of the Eponym Canon and Tiglath-pileser III's lists of annexations and tributaries: Arpad was taken and the kingdom of Bīt-Agusi was annexed to Assyria, while Tarḫulara of Gurgum, Kuštašpi of Kummuḫ, and Sulumal of Melid were allowed to stay on their thrones as Assyrian vassals. 2. The first of the recorded battles took place within the borders of Kummuḫ. It is therefore impossible to interpret the Eponym Canon annotation for 743 as "A defeat on Urarṭu was inflicted in Arpad."[47] It must be understood as a double entry, which is quite common in the Canon. 3. The decisive battle was fought between the towns[48] of Kištan and Ḫalpi. Both were district capitals of the kingdom of Kummuḫ, and therefore towns of a certain importance and located at a certain distance from each other. 4. Though the battle ended with a defeat of Urarṭu, and its allies, it did not result in the immediate destruction of Sarduri's army. The Urarṭians retreated towards their country, fighting on their way several rear guard battles. 5. Tiglath-pileser's pursuit of

44 The sequence—invasion of Urarṭu and shutting up Sarduri II in his capital Ṭurušpa—took place in 735. Here, as in other display inscriptions, events are grouped not chronologically but geographically.

45 *ARAB* I, § 797, with bibliography § 786. Written in 728.

46 *ARAB* I, § 813, with bibliography § 808. Also from 728.

47 As believed by Diakonoff (1951), 307; Tadmor (1961), 254 (he gives credit for it to A. Hildebrand in 1874); Piotrovsky (1969), 83; Shea (1978), 45.

48 Strictly speaking, *Kištan* and *Ḫalpi* are preceded in Tiglath-pileser III's records with KUR, nor URU. It was, however, the standard Assyrian practice to use the determinative KUR when citing territorial units named for their capitals. Besides, Sarduri II, in his text quoted above, explicitly calls Ḫalpi (^URU^*Ḫa-al-pa-ni*) a town, and this should be true for Kištan as well.

the Urarṭians led through an area of high mountains with gorges and precipices. 6. A battle, with heavy casualties for the Urarṭians, occurred at the crossing of the river Sinzi, evidently a major stream. 7. The Urarṭians were able to take most of their baggage and equipment across the river Sinzi and to pitch a camp. At night, the Assyrians launched a surprise attack on the camp, which resulted in a precipitous flight of the Urarṭians and the abandonment of a rich booty to the victors. 8. Sarduri fled on horseback to a pass across the high and steep mountain Sibag. 9. From there he (and, of course, the remnant of his army) reached a bridge on the Euphrates which formed in that area the border of Urarṭu, and safely crossed it. Tiglath-pileser pursued the Urarṭians up to that bridge and no farther—no doubt because it was a floating bridge which the adversary immediately dismantled. 10. The presence in the Urarṭian camp of chariots and of Sarduri's royal coach and ornate bed indicates that, despite the rugged relief of the terrain, the road was suitable for wheel traffic.

All in all, even Tiglath-pileser's boastful description of his victory does not justify such statements of modern authors as "a great pitched battle was fought in which the forces of Urarṭu were utterly routed,"[49] or "quite why the Urarṭian army put up such a poor resistance is not at all clear."[50] The Urarṭian army resisted quite bravely during its long retreat, saved its king from Assyrian captivity, and at least part of it was able to reach its homeland. But where exactly was the arena of this campaign? Can it be put on the map? With the disclosures of the sources quoted above, and sufficient knowledge of the general region in question, the task should not have been very difficult. However, we are dealing in the present case with a remarkable example of how one man's erroneous assertion led astray generations of scholars for three quarters of a century. Most authors who repeated this error did not mention the name of its initiator, and perhaps did not even know it. The interest which Tiglath-pileser III's campaign of 743 has for historical topography and for military history of the ancient Near East makes it worth while to go back to the very roots of the aberration and to straighten it out.

4. W. Belck's Identifications of Kištan and Ḫalpi

It all started in 1902 when the well-known collector and publisher of Urarṭian inscriptions, C.F. Lehmann (later Lehmann-Haupt), made in passing a perfectly justified remark about "the southwestern Chaldian [i.e., Urarṭian] boundary (the Euphrates and the Euphrates bridge in the area of Izoly). . . which is otherwise known from Tiglath-pileser III . . ."[51] For this he was vehemently attacked, two years later, by

49 Gurney (1954), 45.

50 Burney and Lang (1972), 148. It goes without saying that Tiglath-pileser's figure of the enemy's losses—72,950—is just a figure of speech.

51 Lehmann(-Haupt) (1902), 112, with a reference to a 1900 article by Belck in which he said the same thing. For curiosity's sake, we shall quote here the famous geographer Ellsworth Huntington who had visited the area in question in 1901, during his perilous descent of "The Great Cañon of the Euphrates River" on a kelek (raft of inflated skins): "Near Kemur Khan, on the left side, is a cuneiform inscription recounting an expedition of Tiglath Pileser and speaking of a certain bridge, presumably over the Euphrates. Just up-stream from the inscription is a fairly narrow place in the river, with low cliffs on either

his fellow Urarṭologist, Waldemar Belck.[52] Yes, said he, he earlier thought so himself, but Lehmann should have known that more recently

> I have abandoned this previous view of mine as untenable and incompatible with factual conditions, and came instead to the conviction that the bridge mentioned by Tiglath-pileser III has to be sought *in the area of Samosata* . . . It suffices to say that I have found and established *with precision, with full precision*, the battlefield on which, in 743 B.C., the struggle between Assur and Chaldia came to a decision for the first time. Tiglath-pileser III reports that he annihilated the troops of Sardur III in the (in another passage: "between the") fields of *Kištan* and *Ḫalpi*, districts of the land of Kummuḫ (Commagene), and that he pursued Sardur III, who had fled at night on a "mare," up to the bridge of the Euphrates, the boundary of his land. Now, both of these place names still exist today in the region of ancient Kummuḫ-Commagene almost unchanged as *"Küschtam"* and "*Chalfat,*" separated by only a few kilometers, the former a little west of the Euphrates, the latter directly on the Euphrates and about 20-30 kilometers downstream from Samosata.[53]
>
> The recovery of this battlefield settles also the location of the bridge as *south* of the Taurus, for it is unthinkable that Tiglath-pileser could have pursued the retreating Sardur over the wild Taurus, which is here especially difficult to cross and is inhabited by unruly populations, all the way to Malatia and Izoly, i.e. for several days of marching. . . . There can only be question of a bridge *south of the Taurus* and *north of Ḫalfat-Halpi*, which must thus have been located *near*, *or directly at, Samosata* . . . *Tiglath-pileser III provides us thus with the proof that a fixed bridge over the Euphrates at Samosata existed since early antiquity* . . . The Chaldian empire extended much farther south than has been generally accepted till now. Already

side which might readily serve as piers of a bridge" (Huntington [1902], 190). He mistook Sarduri II's inscription for one of his adversary Tiglath-pileser III, but correctly remembered that something was said by the latter about a bridge over the Euphrates used by the former, for which the Izolu-Kömürhan sector of the river would have been the natural location.

52 Belck (1904) 182-4.

53 Belck added here the following footnote full of self-admiration: "Hence, Tiglath-pileser III's expression 'between the fields of Kištan and Ḫalpi' must be understood *literally*—that this great and bloody battle took place between the localities Küschtam and Chalfat. Such precise pinpointing of an important ancient, extra-European battlefield as has been reached here is, to say the least, quite extraordinary; future travelers and explorers will do a good thing by carefully searching for it in the plain between the cited places, where diggings will fairly certainly reveal many military implements from that time."

> Menuas conquered not only Ulliba and Sophene but also the land of Ašurini, i.e., the Til Ašuri of the Assyrians, the later Tela Antoninopolis . . . and the frequently mentioned state of *Šupria* . . . lay directly west of Til Ašuri, its name *has been preserved till now* in that of the town of *Suwerek*.[54]

5. Consequences and Contradictions of W. Belck's Hypothesis

We have included this lengthy excerpt so that it may speak for itself and reveal how tenuous were the premises of Belck's conception. In order to justify his identification of the battle sites of Kištan and Ḫalpi with Küştam and Halfeti (in modern Turkish spelling),[55] he had to condemn the perfectly safe Taurus highway from Melitene to Commagene which linked the two regions since the earliest antiquity, and to transpose the Euphrates crossing to Samosata; this, in turn, required the aprioric assumption that the northernmost part of Mesopotamia was at that time under Urarṭian domination, and the stupendous identification of the Urarṭian ^{KUR}*A-šú-ri-i-ni*[56] (i.e., quite simply, Assyria) with Til-Aššuri (in Media)[57] and the latter with Tela-Antoninopolis (now Viranşehir) in Mesopotamia, and of the land of Šupria (Šubria) in the Sasun Mountains of south central Armenia[58] with modern Siverek northwest of Viranşehir. Belck failed to mention that Halfeti is situated on the *left* bank of the Euphrates; its equation with Ḫalpi, a district capital of Kummuḫ, would thus necessitate to assume that the territory of Kummuḫ extended into Mesopotamia, for which there is no proof whatever. Moreover, the distance between Halfeti and Samsat (Samosata) is not "20-30 kilometers" but 65 km. in airline, across the northwestern corner of Mesopotamia, or over 90 km. along the right bank of the Euphrates. A glance at the map makes one wonder: if Sarduri intended to cross the Euphrates into Mesopotamia, why did he not do it at Halfeti itself rather than undertake a roundabout march along arduous trails to Samosata?[59] Why would a major battle be fought in an area of no strategic importance, with no urban centers and no roads, only bridle paths?[60] And where are the gorges, precipices, and high steep mountains of Tiglath-pileser III's relation? Even though the area between Küştam and the Euphrates is not exactly a "plain," as Belck characterized it, but a

[54] Emphasis and spelling of place names (with its occasional inconsistencies)—as in the German original.

[55] Küştam has been more recently renamed Güder; cf. the map of the Gaziantep vilayet 1:270,000 (Gaziantep Kültür Derneği, 1962), a copy of which was kindly given to me by Prof. U. Bahadir Alkim. Archi, Pecorella, and Salvini, who made an archaeological survey of the Gaziantep region in 1970, knew about the equation of Küştam with Kištan but did not visit it (*Gaziantep*, 39 n. 17)—probably because there was nothing to see there, neither a mound nor ruins.

[56] Also spelled ^{KUR}*Aš-šur/Aš-šur-ni-i/Aš-šur-ni-ni.*

[57] Cf. "Tel-Assar," *IDB*, Suppl. Vol. 868.

[58] Diakonoff (1968), 16-17, 138 *et pass.*; Parpola (1970), map.

[59] See below on precisely such a view by Forrer.

[60] See the detailed description of a horseback ride from Aintab (Gaziantep) to Halfeti via Küştam by Humann ap. Humann and Puchstein (1890), 172-3; the map *Turkey* 1.200,000, sheet G 12 (*Birecik*); and the map quoted in n. 54 above. V. Yorke also rode from ʿAintab to the Euphrates crossing at Halfeti (Khalfat) (Yorke [1896], 320-21). This is the only reason for anybody to enter this corner of Commagene.

terrain of low hills and valleys, its configuration does not correspond to the landscape evoked by the texts.

Were *Halfeti* at least a unique toponym . . . But place names of this kind are quite common in modern Turkey. Besides the *Halfeti* in question (vilayet of Urfa), the *Gazetteer* of Turkey lists *Halfe* (Elâziğ), *Halfeli* (kars), *Halfet* (Ankara); add *Halfan* (Gaziantep); the *Gazetteer* of Syria mentions, in addition, *Ḫalfatlī* (province of Aleppo). Furthermore, Halfeti on the Euphrates was founded about 1880 as a new administrative center (seat of a kaymakam) instead of Rumkale upstream on the opposite bank, and absorbed its population.[61] No mounds or ruins are reported near it, and its very name is not mentioned by early explorers of the Euphrates Valley.[62] As for *Küştam*, cf. *Kiştim* (Erzincan).

But few, if any, of the authors who followed Belck ever submitted his assertion to critical examination. The double consonance *Kištan—Ḫalpi*: *Küştam—Halfeti* had a kind of hypnotic influence on them, and they continued to copy the alleged identity from each other. C.F. Lehmann-Haupt, whom Belck had upbraided for putting Sarduri II's bridge where it actually belonged, was among the first to accept his conception.[63] E. Forrer took the identity of Kištan with Küştam and of Ḫalpi with Halfeti for granted (without giving anybody the credit for it)[64] and went one step further: "Urarṭu made the Syrian princes of Kummuḫu and Arpaddu its dependents and seized for itself the territory on the left bank of the Euphrates south of Kummuḫu, so that Urarṭu bordered on the turtan's province of Ḫarran. In this way it gained a road to Syria which, after crossing the Taurus near Bitlis, continued via Mejafarkin, north of Amedi, Süwerek, and crossed the Euphrates at Ḫalpi (now Ḫalfat)."[65] This construction eliminated the strange detour to Samosata, but introduced a new daring hypothesis—a modification of Belck's—that Urarṭu possessed the northwestern part of Mesopotamia and that Sarduri II's road to Syria led across it. There is not the slightest hint in the documents to show that any king of Urarṭu ever used such an itinerary; it is entirely deduced from the identification of Ḫalpi with Halfeti.[66] Among other authors who explicitly accepted the equation Kištan-Küştam and Ḫalpi-Halfeti we may mention E. Honigmann,[67] S. Smith,[68]

61 Humann pa. Puchstein (1890), 174-5.

62 Such as Chesney (1850), Ainsworth (1842), (1888).

63 Lehmann-Haupt (1910), 482-3.

64 Forrer (1920), 79.

65 *Ibid.*, 85.

66 Forrer's idea that Assyria did not control the northwestern strip of Mesopotamia along the Euphrates till 739, as shown on both maps in (1920), is based on misplacements of certain ancient sites and wrong understanding of a list of Tiglath-pileser III's conquests, *ARAB* I, § 785. But a refutation of it would require an excursus of a length disproportionate to that of the whole article.

67 Honigmann (1923), map of Roman Northern Syria, on which he carefully noted *Küštam* and *Ḫalfati*, even though these places had no relation whatever to the Roman-Byzantine period and are not mentioned in the text of the study. He also approvingly cited Belck's identification in *RE* III A (1929), 233-4, *s.v.* "Singas potamos," but in his comprehensive "Syria," *RE* IV A (1932), 1597, he began to doubt whether Sarduri really crossed the Euphrates at Samosata: perhaps rather at Zeugma (Belkis)—that is *south* of Küştam, which supposes a totally paradoxical line of retreat.

68 S. Smith (1925), 35. On map I, the name *Kummukh* reaches into Mesopotamia almost all the way to Amedi.

P. Naster,[69] I. M. Diakonoff,[70] R. Labat,[71] J. Zablocka,[72] C. Burney and D. M. Lang,[73] G.A. Melikišvili notes it as possible.[74] Without mentioning these towns, Belck's setting for the battle was accepted by A. T. Olmstead,[75] H. Schmöckel,[76] and G. Roux.[77]

6. Urarṭian Evidence on the Location of Ḫalpi

The strange thing about this virtual consensus is that no consideration was taken of the fact that Sarduri II himself provided a very specific and precious topographic datum on one of the two district towns in question. We have already seen that the second of the three "royal cities" (district capitals) of Qumaḫa (Kummuḫ), which Sarduri captured only two or three years before his clash with Tiglath-pileser, was [URU]*Ḫa-al-pa-ni* URU MAN-*nu-si ṣu-i-ni-i-ši-ni*.[78] Now *ṣuinišini* is an adjective derived from the noun *ṣue* "lake," quite common in Urarṭian texts, and can best be rendered as "lacustrine."[79] Applied to *Ḫalpa(ni)*, it indicates that the city stood on a lake, or was located in an area of lakes.[80] The identity of Sarduri's Ḫalpa with Tiglath-pileser's Ḫalpi was recognized by both König and Melikišvili.[81] All that remains to be done is to take a topographic map

69 Naster (1938), 13-17 and map.

70 Diakonoff (1951), 307, n. 1 to document No. 42, and map; (1955): map of Urarṭu opposite p. 516; map of Assyria *ca.* 654 B.C. opposite p. 556; on map of Assyria in the ninth century B.C., pp. 536-537, a strip of land *ca.* 25 km. wide along the left bank of the Euphrates is included in the borders of Kummuḫ.

71 Labat (1967), 52.

72 Zablocka (1971), map II opposite p. 80 (only Kištan shown). Also, "Sakce Gözu" (1950), 69; "Ḫalpi and Kishtan (Halfati and Kuştam) in Kummuḫ."

73 Burney and Lang (1972), 148: "Tiglath-pileser III won a victory over Sarduri II at Halpa (Halfeti, not Aleppo) on the banks of the Euphrates."

74 Melikišvili (1960), 429.

75 Olmstead (1923) 182-3: "The coalition chose a position in the rough hills on the northwest corner of Mesopotamia, in the district of Qummuh. The Sinzi canal was dyed with their blood, and Sarduri eluded pursuit by a solitary flight on a mare . . . Chase was continued to the boundary of Chaldia proper, the bridge across the Euphrates . . . " There are no rough hills nor canals in the northwest corner of Mesopotamia, and the question arises as to why Sarduri, who was already on the eastern bank of the Euphrates had to recross it in order to reach "Chaldia proper." In a later work, (1931), 433, Olmstead completely omitted any geographical data on that battle.

76 Schmöckel (1957), 262: "The clash took place in the territory of [Kummuḫ]; it ended in a total victory of the Assyrians and the precipitous flight of Sardur beyond the river," with a reference to Belck (a debt no other Assyriologist paid him).

77 Roux (1964) 279: "Sardur . . . was defeated near Samsat, on the Euphrates, and fleeing ignominously on a mare, 'escaped at night and was seen no more.'" It is curious how often modern authors repeat the Assyrian cliché about fleeing on a mare while paying little attention to more important aspects of the campaign. In the turmoil and darkness of the night, who could tell the sex of Sarduri's mount unless he was captured while riding it?

78 UKN 155, E, 50-51 (HCI 103, § 9, IV, 56-57).

79 See Melikišvili (1960), 405-06, list of all occurrences of *ṣue* in Urarṭian royal inscriptions, and structural analysis of *ṣuinišini* "lacustrine" (*ozërnyj*), "(rich in) lakes." Same, König (1955), 200. It is important to remember that *ṣue* means only "lake," never "river," for which the Urarṭians used the ideogram ÍD.

80 Cf. König (1955), 124 n. 4: "It is only clear that a lake (*ṣue*) had some importance for Ḫalpa."

81 König (1955), 123 n. 4; Melikišvili (1960), 429 *s.v. Ḫalpa*.

of the relevant area of Turkey and to find which of its lakes (if any) could possess on its shore a district city accessible to large armies with chariots and waggons. The map *Adiyaman (Turkey* 1:200,000, sheet F 12) shows indeed two lakes within the territory of ancient Kummuḫ.[82] One of them is Abdulharap Gölü, near the village of Çelikhan, 30 km. north of Adiyaman, high in the Taurus, on a bridle path that connects Adiyaman with Malatya. The trail is extremely difficult and is never used for travel between the two cities.[83] The other lake is Gölbaşi, which is the northeasternmost of three lakes formed by the upper Aksu, a tributary of the Ceyhan (Pyramus). It is located at an important road junction of great strategic value. The highway from Maraş (ancient Marqasi, capital of Gurgum) to Malatya (near ancient Melid) follows the Aksu valley, crosses the Göksu (a tributary of the Euphrates) 12 km. northeast of the Gölbaşi Lake, goes up to the Reşadiye Pass, turns sharply to the northwest to Sürgü and Doğanşehir across a plateau, reaches the valley of the Sultansu and descends into the plain of Melitene west of Malatya. This is a relatively easy route which, long before it was improved and paved, could be used by an army which included cavalry and artillery.[84] At the northeastern extremity of Lake Gölbaşi begins a road to Besni and Adiyaman and from there to Samsat, the site of the ancient capital of Kummuḫ and Commagene. From Besni (the medieval fortress of Bahasna), a road which played an important role in Roman and medieval times led to Aleppo via Keysun, Araban, and Gaziantep (ʿAintab).[85] And on the eastern shore of Lake Gölbaşi, H.H. von der Osten noted and photographed an ancient mound.[86] It most perfectly corresponds to the location and description of Ḫalpa in Sarduri II's annals.

7. The Actual Route of Sarduri II's Advance and Retreat

Once this identification is made, many other pieces of the geographical puzzle fall into their places. We have seen that Sarduri II's first invasion of Commagene, in 746 or 745, began by the capture of the border fortress of Uita, which ninety years earlier belonged to Melid but now to Kummuḫ. This opened for him the way to the next important city, Ḫalpa-on-the-lake, which dominated the roads southwestward to Gurgum and southeastward to the captial of Kummuḫ. The location of the third conquered city, Parala, is unknown, but since Sarduri did not leave the territory of Kummuḫ, it may have corresponded to the natural stronghold of Besni (26 km., or a

82 There are no lakes in the southern part of Kummuḫ, covered by sheet G 12 (*Birecik)*.

83 Apparently, it was this trail that the future field marshall H. von Molke reconnoitered in 1838-39, during the Turkish-Egyptian war, and found it "the most exhausting march I have ever made," *Briefe aus der Türkei aus den Jahren 1835-1839*, 8th ed., 312 and 385 f., quoted in Dörner and Naumann (1935), 105 and n. 1. A notion about the forbidding nature of a trail (or trails) further east can be gained from reading the reports of Yorke (1896), 324, and Stark (1966), 170-01.

84 See Sykes (1904), 119-26; von der Osten (1930), 94-7; Dörner and Naumann (1939), 102-07; Honigmann (1954), 37, 136, 155-6; Garelli (1963), 97-8.

85 Marmier (1890), 529; Cumont (1917), 242; Dörner and Naumann (1939), 111; Wagner (1975), 71 (fig. 101), 78.

86 Von der Osten (1930), 94 and fig. 98.

day's march, from Gölbaşi) which controlled the road to Arpad. It was at that juncture that Gurgum and Arpad followed the example of Kummuḫ and paid homage to Urarṭu. Tiglath-pileser III's counter-offensive in Syria began by the siege of Arpad.[87] Its king Mati'-ilu, one may presume, sent an urgent appeal for help to Sarduri who seems to have been prepared for such an eventuality and set out with his troops by the same route as before for the simple reason that this was the only road available.[88] He and his army crossed the Euphrates on a floating bridge[89] from the Urarṭian advanced base, the fortress of Ṭumeški, where the river is quiet and relatively narrow and where there has always been the crossing point from Sophene to Melitene.[90] Sarduri marched through the kingdom of Melid and took along a contingent supplied by his vassal Sulumal. Then he went over the Taurus passes into Commagene, where he was joined by troops of Gurgum and Kummuḫ. But he did not even reach the southern border of Kummuḫ when he was met by the Assyrian army.

As for Tiglath-pileser III, he was not caught by surprise. The fact that the very first clash between his troops and those of Sarduri II took place inside Kummuḫ, shows that he had been forewarned of the Urarṭian advance. From what we know about the efficient Assyrian intelligence service inside Urarṭu under Sargon,[91] we may assume that it already existed under the great organizer Tiglath-pileser III. As soon as he learned that the Urarṭians had crossed the Euphrates, he interrupted the siege of Arpad and led his army to Kummuḫ via Oylum, Gaziantep, Araban, and Keysun. This would explain the puzzling circumstance that four years are annotated in the Eponym Canon as having been devoted to military operations against Arpad (743, 742, 741, 740), but a note under 741 states that "it was conquered after three years." The three years of siege were counted from 742, when it was resumed in earnest.[92] Since we have established that Tiglath-pileser III's Ḫalpi, where the first stage of the fighting ended, was located on Lake Gölbaşi, then Kištan, where it started, must have been situated closer to Arpad. If, furthermore, Besni, as we have conjectured, corresponds to Parala, then a possible site for Kištan could be Keysun, 14 km. south of Besni. We venture this guess

[87] Tiglath-pileser III does not state by which route he marched to Arpad. He could have proceeded either via the Euphrates crossing at Belkis (classical Zeugma, Shalmaneser III's Zuqarru) and Gaziantep (Paqarḫubuna of the Assyrian records), as Adad-nirari III advanced against Atar-šumki of Arpad and his allies (fragment published by Millard and Tadmor [1973], 58), or via Arslan Taš (Assyrian Ḫadattu, where he built himself a palace), the river crossing at Tell Aḥmar (Til Barsib), and Manbiğ (Nampigi), which even in the most critical years of the eighth century remained in Assyrian hands.

[88] When Hall (1957), 462 wrote that "Sarduris . . . unexpectedly marched down the Euphrates gorges to attack the Assyrian advance in flank," he ascribed to Sarduri a feat that is physically impossible to perform. On the total impassability of the great Euphrates gorge through the Taurus see Huntington (1903) and Mitford (1974), 175 n. 103.

[89] Even the Romans, the foremost bridge constructors of the ancient world, never attempted to span the Euphrates, in any point, by a permanent bridge.

[90] Cf. Strabo on Tomisa (n. 15 above) and Ammianus Marcellinus XVIII, 7, 10, on Barzalo and Claudias (which should be located, across the river from, respectively, Kömürhan and Izolu).

[91] E.g. ABL 101, 123, 145, 148, 251, 380, 381, 424, 444, 515 (also in transliteration and translation, in Waterman [1930-36], same numeration); more letters of this kind published by Saggs (1958).

[92] Otherwise Shea (1978), 45.

not because of the slight assonance of the names[93] but because Keysun stands on a large mound which testifies to the existence there of a sizable ancient city, on an intersection of two ancient roads including the one by which Tiglath-pileser III marched northward, and played a considerable role as a fortress during Arab–Byzantine wars of the early Middle Ages.[94] Assuming, as a hypothesis, that the Urarṭian and the Assyrian troops made their first contact at Keysun, it is interesting to find what distance each of them had covered before reaching it. For Sarduri's army, the itinerary from Hatipuşaği to Keysun amounted to approximately 210 km.[95] Because of the rugged character of much of the route, the average length of a day's march was probably no more than 20 km. The march would therefore have required ten or eleven days. Tiglath-pileser's army had to traverse ca. 150 km. from Arpad to Keysun,[96] through a much easier terrain, and it could have covered it in six days.

The first engagement resulted in a retreat of the Urarṭian army which had now to retrace its whole way. We can easily imagine that when it reached the crossroads of Besni, the contingent of Kummuḫ broke away from it and fled in the direction of its capital, and that the contingent of Gurgum did the same at Ḫalpi whence the Aksu valley road led to their country. Then came the crossing of the deep and rapid Göksu River. Its name in classical times was *Singas,*[97] and credit must be given to E. Honigmann for identifying with it Tiglath-pileser III's [ÍD]*Si-in-zi* and suggesting the possibility that the last sign of the name, *zi*, is a writing error for the almost identical sign *gi*.[98] True, he still thought, following Belck, that Sarduri retreated to Samosata, and placed therefore his crossing of Sinzi/Singas/Göksu not far from its confluence with the Euphrates. But the crossing of the upper Göksu by the road to Malatya is equally ancient,[99] and it is there that another rear guard battle took place. The "high and steep mountain Sibag," where Sarduri fled after the Assyrian attack on his camp, is the southern ridge of the Taurus system, which has to be ascended by the Reşadiye (or Erkenek) Pass in order to reach the central plateau and the descent into the plain of Malatya.[100] Having attained that plain, Sarduri was abandoned by the last of his reluctant allies, the troops of Melid, but he and his Urarṭians were able to keep ahead of the

[93] Turkish *Keysun* derives from Arabic *Kaysūm* (Syriac *Kayšūm* or *Kaysūm*), and this, in turn, from Roman *Cesum* (thus in the Peutinger Table), which is probably a simplified spelling of Latin *caesum* "cutting" (through a forest). Roman military camps in Syria were sometimes given Latin names.

[94] Cf. Yaqūt IV, 333 = Le Strange (1890), 475; Honigmann (1935), index *s.v. Kaêsoun*; von der Osten (1930), 135-6; Dörner and Naumann (1939), 110-11.

[95] *Viz.*, Hatipuşagi 49 km. Malatya 74 km. Reşadiye Pass 46 km. Gölbaşi 26 km. Besni 14 km. Keysun. Total 209 km.

[96] *Viz.*, Tell Rif'at (Arpad) 27 km. Oylum 50 km. Gaziantep 48 km. Araban 20 km. Keysun. Total 145 km.

[97] The identity of Singas with Göksu is certain; see Dörner and Naumann (1939), 107-08, 111-12.

[98] Honigmann, *RE* III A (1929), 233-4.

[99] Remains of an ancient bridge near Perveri: Ainsworth (1842), I 262; Sykes (1904), 124.

[100] Descriptions of the pass: Ainsworth (1842), I, 160-61; Sykes (1904), 120-24. We normalize *Sibag* rather than *Sibak* because similar place names existed in southeastern Anatolia during the Roman period: *Sebagênê* on the western slope of the Anti-Taurus; *Sobagênê*, ancient name of Hurman Kalesi in Cataonia; *Sabagênê*, which Ptolemy placed in the Taurus between Melitene and Commagene, near Zizoatra (= Zibaṭra, now Doğanşehir on the Maraş-Malatya highway). Ptolemy's geography of southeastern Anatolia is not very accurate, but if he did not misplace his *Sabagênê* from somewhere else, its name may have perpetuated Tiglath-pileser III's *Sibag*. On these places, cf. Ramsay (1890), index, *s.vv.*

pursuing Assyrians and to reach, cross, and dismantle the bridge on the Euphrates to what, as Tiglath-pileser conceded, was Sarduri's own country. Tiglath-Pileser did not overtake Sarduri, but his appearance in Melitene re-established at least, after a long interval, Assyrian political presence in that region.

Thus ended the short-lived Urarṭian interference in Syria and began its relentless conquest and absorption by the revitalized Assyrian Empire. Tiglath-pileser III's campaign of 743, which had historic consequences and for which we possess a relatively good documentation, deserves to be perceived in its proper geographical and strategic setting.[101]

[101] A newly recovered and as yet unpublished fragment of a stele of Tiglath-pileser III (Louis D. Levine, *Two Neo-Assyrian Stelae from Iran*, Toronto 1972, pp. 11-24), apparently contains a fifth report of the campaign against Sarduri II.

References

Ainsworth, W. F.

1842 *Travels and Researches in Asia Minor, Mesopotamia, Chaldea, and Armenia.* Two vols. London.

1888 *A Personal Narrative of the Euphrates Expedition.* Two vols. London.

Albright, W. F.

1956 "The Nebuchadnezzar and Neriglissar Chronicles." *BASOR* No. 143, 28-33.

Belck, W.

1904 "Die Steleninschrift Rusas' II Argistiḫinis von Etschmiadzin." *ZDMG* 58, 161-197.

Beran, T.

1957 "Zur Inschrift Sardurs III bei Izoli." *Istanbuler Mitteilungen* 7, 133-145.

Bittel, K.

1950 *Grundzüge der Vor- und Frühgeschichte Klein-Asiens.* 2nd ed. Tübingen.

Bossert, H. T.

1951 "Zur Geschichte von Karkamis." *Studi Classici e Orientali* 1, 35-67.

Burney, C. and Lang, D. M.

1972 *The Peoples of the Hills: Ancient Ararat and Caucasus.* New York.

Cantineau, J.

1931 "Remarques sur la stèle araméenne de Sefiré-Soudjin." *RA* 28, 167-78.

Chesney, F. R.

1850 *The Expedition for the Survey of the Rivers Euphrates and Tigris . . . in the years 1835, 1836, and 1837* . . . Vols. I, II, and vol of maps. London.

Diakonoff, I. M.

1951 "Assiro-vavilonskie istočniki po istorii Urartu" [Assyro-Babylonian sources on the history of Urartu]. Supplements to *VDI,* 1951, Nos. 1-3.

1955 Chapters XX, 1 and XXI in *Vsemirnaja istorija* [World history], I, 513-26, 534-59. Moscow.

1968 *Predystorija armjanskogo naroda: istorija Armjanskogo nagor'ja s 1500 po 500 g. do n. è.: xurrity, luvijcy, protoarmjane* [Protohistory of the Armenian people: History of the Armenian upland from 1500 to 500 B.C.: Hurrians, Luwians, Proto-Armenians]. Erevan.

Donner, H.

1970 "Adadnirari III. und die Vassalen des Westens." *Ap. Archäologie und Altes Testament: Festschrift für Kurt Galling,* ed. by A. Kuschke and E. Kutsch, 49-59. Tübingen.

Dörner, F. K. und Naumann, R.
1939 *Forschungen in Kommagene* (Istanbuler Forschungen 10). Berlin.
Dupont-Sommer, A.
1956 "Une inscription araméenne inédite de Sfiré." *Bulletin du Musée de Beyrouth* 13, 23-41.
Forrer, E.
1920 *Die Provinzeinteilung* des assyrsichen Reiches. Leipzig.
Garelli, P.
1963 *Les Assyriens en Cappadoce* (Bibl. archéol. et hist. de l'Inst. Français d'Archéol. d'Istanbul , XIX). Paris.
Garelli, P., et Nikiprowetzky, V.
1974 *Le Proche-Orient asiatique: Les empires mésopotamiens, Israël* (Nouvelle Clio 2a). Paris.
Garstang, J. and Gurney, O. R.
1959 *The Geography of the Hittite Empire* (Occ. Publ. of the Brit. Inst. of Archaeol. in Ankara, No. 5). London.
Gazetteer No. 104: Syria: Official Standard Names, approved by the U.S. Board on Geographic Names. Washington 1967.
Gazetteer No. 46: Turkey: Official Standard Names, approved by the U. S. Board on Geographic Names. Washington 1960.
Gaziantep, A. Archi, P.E. Pecorella, M. Salvini
Gaziantep e la sua regione: Uno studio storico e topografico degli insediamenti preclassici (Incunabula Graeca, XLVIII). Rome 1971.
Goetze, A.
1957 *Kleinasien*. 2d revised edition. (Handbuch der Altertumswissenschaft, 3/1/3/3/1). Munich.
Gurney, O. R.
1954 *The Hittites*. 2nd ed. Harmondsworth.
Hall, H. R.
1957 *The Ancient History of the Near East*, 11th ed. New York.
Hawkins, J. D.
1970 "Hieroglyphic Hittite Inscriptions of Commagene." *AnSt* 20, 69-110, pl. VII-XVIII.
1972 "Building Inscriptions of Carchemish: The Long Wall of Sculpture and Great Staircase." *AnSt* 22, 87-114, 1 pl.
1973 Review of E. Orthmann, *Untersuchungen zur späthethitischen Kunst. ZA* 63, 307-311.
1974a "Assyrians and Hittites." *Iraq* 36, 67-83.
1974b *RLA* IV: "Ḫatti: The First Millennium B.C.," 152-9.
Honigmann, E.
1923 *Historische Topographie von Nordsyrien im Altertum*. Leipzig [reprint from *ZDPV* 46 (1923), 149-93, 47 (1924), 1-64].
1935 *Die Ostgrenze des Byzantinischen Reiches* (A. A. Vasiliev, *Byzance et les Arabes*, III). Brussels.

1954a *Le couvent de Barṣauma et le patriarcat jacobite d'Antioche et de Syrie* (Corpus scriptorum christianorum orientalium, vol. 146: Subsidia, tome 7). Louvain.

1954b *RE* III AL "Singas potamos," 233-4.- *RE* IV A: "Syria," 1549-1727.

Houwink ten Cate, Ph. H. J.

1967 "Kleinasien zwischen Hethitern und Persern," Ch. 2 of *Fischer Weltgeschichte*, IV, 112-34. Frankfurt am Main.

Humann, K. und Puchstein, O.

1890 *Reisen in Kleinasien und Nordsyrien* . . . Two vols. Berlin.

Huntington, E

1902 "Through the Great Cañon of the Euphrates River." *The Geographical Journal* 20, 175-200.

Kinnier Wilson, J. V.

1972 *The Nimrud Wine Lists: A study of men and administration at the Assyrian capital in the Eighth Century, B.C.* (CTN 1). London.

König, F. W.

1955 *Handbuch der chaldischen Inschriften (AfO* Beiheft 8). Graz.

Labat, R.

1967 "Assyrien und seine Nachbarländer (Babylonien, Elam, Iran) von 1000 bis 617 v. Chr. / Das neubabylonische Reich bis 539 v. Chr." Ch. 1 of *Fischer Weltgeschichte*, IV, 9-111, 341-6. Frankfurt am Main.

Laessøe, J.

1959 "A Statue of Shalmaneser III, From Nimrud." *Iraq* 21, 147-57, pl. XL-XLII.

Laroche, E.

1966 *Les noms des Hittites.* Paris.

Lehmann(-Haupt), C. F.

1902 "Die neugefundene Steleninschrift Rusas' II von Chaldia." *ZDMG* 56, 101-15.

1910 *Armenien einst und jetzt*, vol. I. Berlin.

Le Strange, G.

1890 *Palestine Under the Moslems: A Description of Syria and the Holy Land from A.D. 650 to 1500.* London.

Lloyd, S.

1956 *Early Anatolia*. Harmondsworth.

Loon, M. van

1974 "The Euphrates Mentioned by Sarduri II of Urartu." *Anatolian Studies Presented to H. G. Güterbock* . . . ed. by K. Bittel, Ph. H. J. Houwink ten Cate, and E. Reiner (Uitgaven van het Nederlands Hist.-Archaeol. Inst. te Istanbul, XXXV). Istanbul.

Malamat, A

1976 "A New Proposal for the Identification of KTK in the Sefire Inscriptions" (Hebrew). *Ap.* M. Razin, *Census Lists and Genealogies and Their Historical Implications*, Haifa, VII-Xi.

Marmier, G.

1890 "La route de Ṣamosate au Zeugma." *Bulletin de la Société de géographie de l'Est,* 12, 518-535.

Melikišvili, G. A.

1960 *Urartskie klinoobraznyje nadpisi* [*Urartian cuneiform inscriptions*]. Moscow.

Meriggi, P.

1953 "Le iscrizioni storiche in eteo geroglifico." *Studi Classici e Orientali* 2, 5-64.

1967 *Manuale di eteo geroglifico: Parte II - Testi - 1ª serie: I testi neo-etei più o meno completi. Rome.*

1975 Same work, *2ª e 3ª serie.*

Meyer, Ed.

1931 *Geschichte des Altertums*. Vol. II, part 2. 4th ed. [Reprint 1965]. Stuttgart.

Millard, A. R. and Tadmor, H.

1973 "Adad-nirari III in Syria: Another Stele Fragment and the Dates of his Campaigns." *Iraq* 35, 57-64, pl. XXIX.

Naster, P.

1938 *L'Asie Mineure et l'Assyrie aux VIIIe et VIIe siècles av. J.-C. d'après les Annales des Rois Assyriens* (Bibl. du *Muséon,* 8). Louvain.

Oded, B.

1972 "The Campaigns of Adad-nirari III into Southern Syria and Palestine" (Hebrew). *Meḥaqrîm be-tōledôt ʿam-Yiśrā'ēl we-'Ereṣ-Yiśra'el*, 25-34. Haifa.

Olmstead, A. T.

1923 *History of Assyria*. New York - London.

1931 *History of Palestine and Syria to the Macedonian Conquest*. New York - London.

Osten, H. H. von der

1930 *Explorations in Hittite Asia Minor, 1929 (OIC* No. 8). Chicago.

Page, S.

1968 "A Stela of Adad-Nirari III and Nergal-Ereš from Tell al Rimah." *Iraq* 30, 139-53, pl. XXXVII-XXXIX.

Parpola, S.

1970 *Neo-Assyrian Toponyms* (AOAT 6). Kevelaer and Neukirchen-Vluyn.

Piotrovsky, B. B.

1969 *The Ancient Civilization of Urartu*. Transl. from the Russian by J. Hogarth. New York/Geneva.

Ramsey, W. M.

1890 *The Historical Geography of Asia Minor* (Royal Geogr. Soc., Suppl. Papers, IV). London.

Rost, P.

1893 *Die Keilschrifttexte Tiglat-Pilesers III* . . . Two vols. Leipzig.

Roux, G.

1966 *Ancient Iraq*. Harmondsworth.

Saggs, H. W. F.

1958 "The Nimrud Letters, 1952—Part IV." *Iraq* 20, 182-212, pl. XXXVIII-XLI.

"Sakce Gözu"

1950 J. du Plat Taylor, M.V. Seton Williams and J. Waechter, "The Excavations at Sakce Gözu." *Iraq* 12, 53-138, Pl. XXV.

Salvini, M.
1972 "Le testimonianze storiche urartee sulle regioni del medio Eufrate: *Melitênê, Kommagênê, Sophênê, Tomisa." La Parola del Passato*, fasc. 142-144, 100-11.

Sayce, A. H.
1925 "The Kingdom of Van (Urarṭu)," Ch. VIII of *CAH,* III, 169-86.

Schmökel, H.
1957 *Geschichte des alten Vorderasien* (Hanbuch der Orientalistik, vol. II, part 3). Leiden.

Shea, W. H.
1978 "Menahem and Tiglath-pileser III." *JNES* 37, 43-9.

Smith, S.
1925 [The Neo-Assyrian Empire]: Chs. I-V of *CAH*, III, 1-131.

Stark, F.
1966 *Rome on the Euphrates: The Story of a Frontier*. New York.

Sykes, M.
1904 *Dar-ul-Islam: A Record of a Journey through Ten of the Asiatic Provinces of Turkey*. London.

Tadmor, H.
1961 "Azriyau of Yaudi." *Scripta Hierosolymitana* 8, 232-71.
1967 "Introductory Remarks to a New Edition of the Annals of Tiglath-pileser III." *Proceedings of the Israel Academy of Sciences and Humanities*, II, No. 9, 168-87.
1973 "The Historical Inscriptions of Adad-nirari III." *Iraq* 35, 141-50.
1975 "Assyria and the West: The Ninth Century and its Aftermath." *Unity and Diversity*, ed. by H. Goedicke and J. J. M. Roberts, 36-48. Baltimore.

Ungnad, A.
— *RLA* II: "Eponymen," 412-57.

Wagner, J.
1975 "Die Römer am Euphrat." *Antike Welt* 6 (Sondernummer: Kommagene), 68-82.

Waterman, L.
1930-36 *Royal Correspondence of the Assyrian Empire*. Four vols. (University of Michigan Studies, XVII-XX). Ann Arbor, Michigan.

Weidner,E. F.
1933 "Der Staatsvertrag Aššurnirâris VI. von Assyrien mit Mati'ilu von Bît-Agusi." *AfO* 8, 17-34.

Wiseman, D. J.
1956 *Chronicles of the Chaldaean Kings (626-556) in the British Museum*. London.

York, V.W.
1896 "A Journey in the Valley of the Upper Euphrates." *The Geographical Journal* 8, 317-35, 453-74, map.

Zabłocka, J.
1971 *Stosunki agrarne w państwie Sargonidów* [Agrarian relations in the Sargonid State] (Uniwersytet im. Adama Mickiewicza, Wydział filozoficzno-historyczny. Seria historia Nr. 47). Poznań.